THAT
TREMENDOUS
LOVE

THAT TREMENDOUS LOVE

An anthology of inspirational quotations, poems,
prayers, and philosophical comments

Edited by

Bishop Fulton J. Sheen, Ph.D., D.D.

Harper & Row, Publishers,
New York, Evanston, and London

Acknowledgment is made to the following for permission to reprint copyrighted material:

ABINGDON PRESS for extracts from *Constructive Aspects of Anxiety* by Seward Hiltner and Karl Menninger, copyright © 1963.

BURNS & OATES, LTD. for extract from *Love and Marriage* by Gustave Thibon, copyright © 1947; (for Canada) for extracts from *Pastoral Sermons* by Ronald Knox; extract from *The Question of Mary* by René Laurentine, trans. by I. G. Pidoux.

BURNS, OATES & WASHBOURNE for extract from *The Church* by A. G. Sertillanges, copyright © 1922.

THE STUDENT CHRISTIAN MOVEMENT PRESS, LTD. for extract from *Law and Love* by T. E. Jessop.

THE CLARENDON PRESS for poems by John Donne and Christina Georgina Rossetti from the *Oxford Book of English Mystical Verse*, copyright 1917.

COLLINS-PUBLISHERS (for Canada) for extracts from *The Phenomenon of Man* by Teilhard de Chardin, copyright © 1959; extract from *The Seven Swords* by Gerald Vann, O.P.

CONTENTS

THAT
TREMENDOUS
LOVE

LOVE
AND THE
WORLD

*The real test of the Christian is not
how much he loves his friends,
but how much he loves his enemies.*
FJS*

HOW LOVE GROWS

At the beginning one loves God for only his gifts or for the emotions He sends us. He treats us then, "like a young woman who is being courted." If gifts are no longer given in abundance after true marriage has occurred it is not because the husband's love is less, but because it is greater. For now he gives himself. It is not the husband's gifts that his wife loves nor his compliments, nor even the thrill of pleasure she gets from his company. She loves *him*. The moment the Lover is loved for Himself, then the nature of the gifts ceases to matter. If God withdraws all sensible gifts it is only because He wants the union between the soul and Himself to be more personal and less dependent on His generosity.

FJS

LOVE IS UNIVERSAL

The father of a ten year old boy, blind practically from birth, took the child from Britanny to Lourdes, there to pray "Lord give sight to my son!" During the Stations of the Cross, suddenly the child could see. He turned his eyes to his father and saw his face for the first time ; and his first words were : "Fine! Everybody's here!" Is that not a parable of what will happen at the end, when many people's eyes will be opened at last and they will see their Father's Face? Overwhelmed by God's goodness, will they not say, "Fine! Everybody's here!"

YVES CONGAR

2

THE ANGLE OF LOVE

There are situations in which a man's capacity for indignation is a test of his *love*. There are enormities against which love cannot help standing out with all its potencies, and some which only love has the courage to challenge. To the pharisees Jesus brought not peace, but a sword, knowing that in the end He would be worsted on the gallow; but the future weal of mankind mattered more to His love than the vested interest of the pharisees or His own skin. He would love everybody, but how could love show only its gentler side to those who not only rejected Him but tried by every device of hate to put obstacles between Him and everybody else? The one thing the love of mankind, for all its preference for gentleness, cannot tolerate is the hate, contempt, or exploitation of mankind. Before this it will erupt like a volcano. The very reason is that it is the *love* of mankind.

T. E. JESSOP

THE LOVE OF CHRIST

Some people learn to love the whole world through the love of God; for them the way of sacrifice is direct and informed with joy. Others learn to love God through loving one another. . . . The heart that has been exchanged for Christ's Heart radiates from the love of its own children to all of the children of God, because now it cannot fail to love the Heavenly Father Himself as Christ loves Him.

CARYLL HOUSELANDER

 3

THE FRIENDS OF LOVE

St. Teresa de Avila exclaimed, "Oh Lord when will You stop spreading difficulties under our feet like this?" "Do not complain, daughter," replied the Divine Master, "that is the way I always treat my friends." St. Teresa answered, "Yes, Lord, and that is why you have so few."

FJS

LOVE AND CHILDREN

You may give them your love but not your thoughts,
For they have their own thoughts.
You may house their bodies but not their souls,
For their souls dwell in the house of tomorrow,
Which you cannot visit, not even in your dreams.

KAHLIL GIBRAN

SUPPOSE

Suppose you had to pass your eternity with Absolute Truth, which you called "relative" on earth? Suppose you had to live with the King of Kings, Whom you dethroned in time, and you had to live with the Spirit of Love on which you turned your back for the thrill of sex —would not such a heaven be a Hell to you?

FJS

God punishes us by leaving us to ourselves forever.
In hell it is our ego that burns.

FJS

A FATHER'S LOVE

Build me a son, O Lord, who will be strong enough to know when he is weak, and brave enough to face himself when he is afraid ; one who will be proud and unbending in honest defeat, and humble and gentle in victory.

Build me a son whose wishbone will not be where his backbone should be ; a son who will know Thee—and that to know himself is the foundation stone of knowledge.

Lead him, I pray, not in the path of ease and comfort, but under the stress and spur of difficulties and challenge. Here, let him learn to stand up in the storm ; here, let him learn compassion for those who fail.

Build me a son whose heart will be clear, whose goal will be high ; a son who will master himself before he seeks to master other men ; one who will learn to laugh, yet never forget how to weep ; one who will reach into the future, yet never forget the past.

And after all these things are his, add, I pray, enough of a sense of humor, so that he may always be serious, yet never take himself too seriously. Give him humility, so that he may always remember the simplicity of true greatness, the open mind of true wisdom, the meekness of true strength. Then I, his father, will dare to whisper : ''I have not lived in vain.''

GENERAL DOUGLAS A. MAC ARTHUR

 5

LOVE FOR YOUR NEIGHBORS

The time has come . . . for us to start using not just the words of peace, but also the works of peace. We . . . know that we can perform the works of peace, because that is what we have been doing (since we were founded in 1957). We simply go out and take care of sick people in parts of the world where medical care is almost entirely unknown. We take care of them simply and unselfishly. By our deeds, and not by words, we demonstrate what is really in the hearts of the American people. We don't stand up on a platform and talk to them through microphones and loudspeakers. We go into an Asian village and live with the people. We treat their ills, we help to deliver their babies, we go to their weddings, we attend their funerals. We speak to them in a language that they can understand. We don't have to tell them we love them. They know we love them, because if we didn't love them we wouldn't be there ministering to their pathetic needs. Thus, they grow to love us, not just as individuals, but as living symbols of America—the only America they really know. That is why I believe that we are restoring genuine meaning to words like ''freedom'' and ''democracy'' and ''love'' for the people of Southeast Asia.

DR. THOMAS A. DOOLEY

LOVE: RADIANT ENERGY OF THE UNIVERSE

Love alone is capable of uniting living beings in such a
way as to complete and fulfill them, for it alone takes
them and joins them by what is deepest in themselves.
This is a fact of daily experience. At what moment do
lovers come into the most complete possession of
themselves if not when they say they are
lost in each other.

... the goal of ourselves, the acme of our originality, is
not our individuality but our person ; and according to
the evolutionary structure of the world we can find our
person only by uniting together. There is no mind without
synthesis. The same law holds good from top to bottom.
The true ego grows in inverse proportion to egoism.
TEILHARD DE CHARDIN

LOVE BEGS

If thou wouldst learn, not knowing how to pray,
Add but a faith, and say as beggars say :
"Master, I'm poor, and blind, in great distress,
Hungry, and lame, and cold, and comfortless ;
Oh succour him that's gravell'd on the shelf
Of pain, and want, and cannot help himself ;
Cast down thine eye upon a wretch, and take
Some pity on me, for sweet Jesus' sake" ;
But hold ! take heed this clause be not put in,
"I never begged before, nor will again."
FRANCIS QUARLES

 7

THE CRY TO BE TESTED

Batter my heart, three person'd God ; for, you
As yet but knock, breathe, shine, and seek to mend ;
That I may rise, and stand, o'erthrow me, and bend
Your force, to break, blow, turn and make me new.
I, like an usurpt town, to another due,
Labour to admit you, but Oh, to no end,
Reason your viceroy in me, me should defend,
But is captiv'd, and proves weak or untrue.
Yet dearly 'I love you,' and would be loved fain,
But am betroth'd unto your enemy :
Divorce me, untie, or break that knot again,
Take me to you, imprison me, for I
Except you, enthrall me, never shall be free,
Nor ever chaste, except you ravish me.

JOHN DONNE

LOVE AND SOLITUDE

Who sits in solitude and is quiet has escaped three wars :
hearing, speaking, seeing ; yet against one thing shall he
continually battle : that is, his own heart.

ABBOT ANTHONY

Here on earth, we have already both Hell and Heaven—
in our passions and in our experience of God.

FATHER YELCHANINOV

The Christian is far more pagan than he knows ; the
pagan is more Christian than he admits.

ROSALIND MURRAY

 9

SPIRIT
OF LOVE

Joy is the happiness of love—love aware of its
own inner happiness. Pleasure comes from
without, but joy comes from within, and it is,
therefore, within the reach of everyone in the
world. For if there is sadness in our hearts,
it is because there is not enough love. But to be
loved, we must be lovable; to be lovable, we must
be good; to be good, we must know Goodness; and
to know Goodness, is to love God, and neighbor,
and everybody in the world.

FJS

LOVE AND LONELINESS

What we need is real love of real people, to heal our loneliness; and that means seeing them as they really are, and loving them that way; and that in turn means not worshipping them as flawless ideals and deities, but helping them, and being helped by them to worship God.

GERALD VANN, O.P.

LOVE OF NEIGHBOR

Since Christ came on earth as man's ideal in the flesh, it has become as clear as daylight what the last and highest stage of the evolution of personality must be. It is this: that, when evolution is finished, at the very point where the end is reached, man finds out, understands and is convinced with all the force of his nature, that the highest use he can make of his personality, of the full flowering of his *self*, is to do away with it, to give it wholly to any and everybody, without division or reserve. This is sovereign happiness. Thus the law of "me" is fused with the law of mankind; and "I" and "all" (in appearance two opposite extremes), each suppressing itself for the sake of the other, reach the highest peak of the individual development, each one separately.

DOSTOEVSKI

RELIGION AND LOVE

Hate and love spring from the same passion, as laughter and sorrow drink from the same fountain of tears. The difference is in the motive and the end for which they live. Religion is something that must be either hated or loved. It cannot be watched.

FJS

WHAT I LOVE

But what do I love when I love Thee? Not beauty of bodies, nor the fair harmony of time, nor the brightness of the light, so gladsome to our eyes, nor sweet melodies of varied songs, nor the fragrant smell of flowers, and ointments, and spices, not manna and honey, not limbs acceptable to embracements of the flesh. None of these I love, when I love my God; and yet I love a kind of light and melody, fragrance, meat, embracement of my inner man : where there shineth into my soul, what space cannot contain, and there soundeth, what time beareth not away and there smelleth, what breathing disperseth not, and there tasteth, what eating diminisheth not, and there clingeth, what satiety divorceth not. This is what I love, when I love my God.

ST. AUGUSTINE

13

BLESSED LOVE

The difference between people who never get the
''breaks'' and those who make every *now* an occasion
for thanking God is this : the latter live in an area of love
greater than their desire to ''have their way'' as a waif
on the street suffers misfortunes which the child in the
loving family does not know, so the man who does not
learn to place full trust in God suffers reverses and
disasters which would not appear as troubles to loving
souls. The sunlight has no favorites, but it cannot shine
as well on a dusty mirror as on a polished one.

FJS

LOVE IS SERVICE

Those who are called to command in this world, as well as
those who are compelled to obey, no longer consider
themselves as holding a position of superiority, a
transcendent right to impose on others ; but as having a
function to exercise, a duty to fulfill toward them—in
short, to be of use, not to use them, to minister and not
to be ministered unto.

FATHER L. LABERTHONNIÉRE

PRAYER OF A SOLDIER IN FRANCE

My shoulders ache beneath my pack
(Lie easier, Cross, upon His back).

I march with feet that burn and smart
(Tread, Holy Feet, upon My heart).

Men shout at me who may not speak
(They scourge Thy back and smote Thy cheek).

I may not lift a hand to clear
My eyes of salty tears that sear.

(Then shall my fickle soul forget
Thy Agony a bloody sweat)

My rifle hand is stiff and numb
(From Thy pierced palm red rivers come).

Lord, Thou didst suffer more for me
Than all the hosts of land and sea.

So let me render back again
This millionth of Thy gift.   Amen.

JOYCE KILMER

GOD IS LOVE

How life changes its meaning when we see the love of the
flesh as the reflection of the Eternal Light shot through
the prism of time! They who would separate the earthly
sound from the heavenly harp can have no music; they
who believe that love is only the body's breath soon find
love breathes its last and they have made a covenant with
death. But they who see in all earthly beauty the faint
copy of Divine loveliness, they who see in fidelity to every
vow, even when the other is untrue, a proof that God
loves us who are so unlovable, they who, in the face of
their trials, see that God's love ended on a cross, they
who allow the river of their rapture to broaden out the
blended channels of prayer and worship—these will,
even on earth, learn that Love was made flesh and
dwelled amongst us. Thus, Love becomes an ascension
toward that blessed day when the limitless depths of our
souls will be filled with the boundless giving, in one
eternal now, where love is life's eternity and God is Love.
FJS

GOD'S POWERFUL LOVE

The faithful loyal wife whose husband is snatched from
her by death, the mother whose son refuses to visit her
and bless her declining days with filial affection, the
friend who has sacrificed all only to be betrayed by one
for whom he gave all—all these experience the keenest
and bitterest of all human sufferings : the pangs of
unrequited love. Such victims can and really do die of
a broken heart.

But what is this love for another human being, compared
to the love of God for man ? The affection a human heart
bears for another lessens as it multiplies the objects of
its love, just as a river loses its fullness the more it
divides itself into little streams.

But with God there is no decrease of love with the
increase of objects loved, any more than a voice loses its
strength because a thousand ears hear it.

FJS

17

BEYOND HUMAN LOVE

To know a woman in the hour of possession, a man must
first have loved her in the exquisite hour of a dream. To
be loved by man in the hour of possession, a woman must
first want to be loved, fostered, and honored as an ideal.
Beyond all human love is another love; that ''other'' is
the image of the possible; it is that possible that every
man and woman love when they love one another. That
possible becomes real in the blueprint love of Christ and
in that other love of the woman who brings Christ
to us and brings us to Christ, Mary the Mother of God.
FJS

PRAYER OF LOVE

Late have I loved Thee, O Beauty so ancient and so new;
late have I loved Thee! For behold Thou wert within me,
and I outside; and I sought Thee outside and in my
unloveliness fell upon those lovely things that Thou hast
made. Thou wert with me and I was not with Thee. I
was kept from Thee by those things, yet had they not
been in Thee, they would not have been at all. Thou didst
call and cry to me and break open my deafness: and
Thou didst send forth Thy beams and shine upon me and
chase away my blindness: Thou didst breathe fragrance
upon me, and I drew in my breath and do now pant for
Thee: I tasted Thee, and now hunger and thirst for Thee:
Thou didst touch me, and I have burned for Thy peace.
ST. AUGUSTINE

18

LOVE OF GOD AND MAN

There is no claim on the part of the "I" for the "Thou" since the union is freely entered upon by both. The "Thou" calls freely and the "I" responds freely. The only means by which the "I" can attain this end is a union of love. . . . Thus the "I" waits on the good pleasure of the "Thou" and hopes for its coming. The attitude of the "I" is one of full surrender and complete abandonment. The "Thou" on his side is not coerced into union. If he gives himself it is out of love. Thus gratuity is the essence of the relationship of love.

EULALIO R. BALTAZAR

LOVE AND CREATION

Brothers, love the whole of God's creation, all of it down to the very dust. Love each leaf, each ray of God's light, love animals, love plants, love everything. If you love everything, you will understand the mystery of God in things. Once you see this, you will go on understanding it better every day. And eventually you will love the world with a love that includes every single thing. Love animals : God has given them a kind of thought and a tranquil enjoyment. Do not disturb it, do not hurt them, do not spoil their happiness, do not go contrary to God's purposes for them. Love little children especially, for they are innocent as angels ; they are given to us as a sign, to touch and cleanse our hearts.

DOSTOEVSKI

 19

HEALING LOVE

A mother watching surgery on her infant suffers for the child and yet endures it for a greater future good; here the Son is the surgeon who, with a two-edged sword, pierces first His Own Heart before He pierces that of His Mother, as if to blunt the piercing when it touches her.

FJS

THE MOTHER'S LOVE (Mary)

As one searches for the reasons for the universal love of Mary among peoples who do not even know her Son, it is to be found in four instincts deeply embedded in the human heart: affection for the beautiful; admiration for purity; reverence for a Queen; and love of a Mother. All of these come to a focus in Mary.

FJS

THE MYSTERY OF MARY

The mystery of her who, in the words of St. Leo,
"conceived God in her mind before she conceived Him
in her body," gives full meaning to the twofold
presence of Mary in the mystery of salvation: her
presence before God and her presence among men, both
in the fellowship of one life, in one body. Here indeed
two utterances made at Cana find their lasting meaning.
The first is addressed to Christ, telling Him of men's
thirst: "They have no wine"; the second to men, telling
them to hope for God's gift and to give their cooperation:
"Do whatever He tells you."

RENÉ LAURENTIN

TO BE BORN AGAIN

There is nothing in us alien to Christ. We add nothing to
Him when we are reborn in Him, reborn in His Death.
All we do is find ourselves anew in Him. Consequently,
Mary finds in us nothing other than Him, in other words,
nothing that is not herself in her complete surrender to
God and His plan of the fulfillment of all He wills—a
surrender which constitutes her motherhood.

LOUIS BOUYER

GOD'S IDEAL WOMAN

God has two pictures of us : one is what we *are,* and the other is what we *ought to be.* He has the *model* and He has the reality : the blueprint and the edifice, the score of music and the way we play it. God has to have these two pictures because in each and every one of us there is some disproportion and want of conformity between the original plan and the way we worked it out. The image is often blurred, the print is faded. Like unhatched eggs some of us refuse to be warmed by the Divine Love which is so necessary for the incubation to a higher level. We all fall short of what God wants us to be.

There is actually only one person in all humanity of whom God has one picture, and in whom there is a perfect conformity between what He wanted her to be and what she is—and that is Mary, the Mother of Our Lord. But Mary is the equal sign, the Ideal that God has of her, what she is and in the flesh. The Model and the copy are perfect ; she is all that was foreseen, planned and dreamed. The melody of her life is played, just as it was written.

FJS

I speak of this in the holy church of Zurich and in all my writings: I recognize Mary as ever Virgin and holy.

ZWINGLI

MOTHER OF JESUS

Mary is the Mother of Jesus, and the Mother of us all. If Christ is ours, we must be where He is; and where He is we must be also, and all that He has must be ours, and His Mother, therefore, is also ours.

MARTIN LUTHER

ODE TO A QUEEN

When God turned back eternity and was young,
  Ancient of Days, grown little for your mirth
(As under the low arch the land is bright)
  Peered through you, gate of heaven—and saw
    the earth. . . .
Or risen from play at your pale raiment's hem
  God, grown adventurous from all time's repose,
Of your tall body climbed the ivory tower
  And kissed upon your mouth the mystic rose.

G. K. CHESTERTON

DOCTRINE OF THE ASSUMPTION

For myself, I have never doubted the doctrine of the Assumption since I heard it preached forty-four years ago in an Anglican church over at Plymouth. You see, we get it all wrong about body and soul, simply because our minds are dominated by matter. We think it the most natural thing in the world that soul and body should be separated after death; that the body should remain on earth and the soul go to Heaven, once it is purged and assoiled. But it is not a natural thing at all; soul and body were made for one another, and the temporary divorce between them is something out of the way, something extraordinary, occasioned by the Fall. In Our Blessed Lady, not born under the scar of that defeat, human nature was perfectly integrated; body and soul belonged to one another, as one day, please God, yours and mine will . . . . one ship has rounded the headland, one destiny is achieved, one human perfection exists and as we watch it, we see God clearer, see God greater, through this masterpiece of His dealings with mankind.

RONALD KNOX

MARY'S GREAT FAITH

Every step the Lord took toward fulfillment of His godly
destiny, Mary followed in bare faith. Comprehension
came only with Pentecost. . . . What is demanded of us
as demanded of her, is a constant wrestling *in faith* with
the mystery of God and with the evil resistance of the
world. Our obligation is not delightful poetry but granite
faith—more than ever in this age of absolutes in which
the mitigating spell is falling from all things and naked
opposites clash everywhere. The purer we see and
understand the figure of the Mother of God as she is
recorded in the New Testament, the greater the gain for
our Christian lives.

ROMANO GUARDINI

Mary was a Virgin before the Conception and Birth, she
remained a Virgin also at the Birth and after it.

MARTIN LUTHER

A PURE WITNESS TO JESUS' LIFE

Mary has an *apostolic* part to play, not in the sense that like the Apostles she was one of the founders and leaders of the Church, but in the sense that she was, like them, an eye-witness of the Life of Christ, and like them, proclaims what she had actually seen. Mary shared in the Life of Jesus, bore witness to it, and proclaimed also the Word of God to us for our salvation.

MAX THURIAN

KNOT OF THE CORD

He is the Eternal in time, she is the House of the Eternal in time. She is the final meeting place of all humanity and all history. Or, as Coventry Patmore says:

"Knot of the cord
Which binds together all and all unto their Lord."

FJS

27

WOMAN OF SORROWS

Why, then, should not she who gave Him that Body with which He could die, and that Blood which He could pour forth, be remembered, not in adoration, but in veneration, and as long as time endures? But if, along with the God Who is the Man of Sorrows and who entered into His Glory, there is a creature, a Woman of Sorrows who accompanied Him into that glory, then we all have an inspiration to love *through* a cross and *with* it, that we, too, may reign with Christ.

FJS

WHY GOD CHOSE MARY

God looked over the world for an empty heart—but not a lonely heart—a heart that was empty like a flute on which He might pipe a tune—not lonely like an empty abyss, which is filled by death. And the emptiest heart He could find was the heart of a Lady. Since there was no self there, He filled it with His very Self.

FJS

THE BLESSED MOTHER'S GRACE

There are many of us who would not come to Our Lord,
unless we had someone who knows our needs better than
we know ourselves, and who will ask Our Lord for us.
This role of Mary makes her acceptable to everyone.
Those at the marriage table did not need to know she was
the Mother of the Son of God in order to receive the
benefit of her Divine Son. But one thing is certain—no
one will ever call on her without being heard, nor
without being finally led to her Divine Son, Jesus Christ,
for Whose Sake she alone exists—for Whose Sake she was
made pure—and for Whose Sake she was given to us.

FJS

REDEEMED

If Mary, who was sinless, would with joy accept a Sword
from Divine sinlessness, then who of us, who are guilty
of sin, shall ever complain if the same Jesus permits us a
sorrow for the remission of our sins?

FJS

BEHOLD! THE MOTHER OF GOD

It is easier to visualize the Virgin than it is to imagine Christ, and no one will ever be able to understand how the Divine Nature imprinted, or, on the contrary, disguised its sign on the face of a man. But if it is impossible to imagine a God-Man, it is easy to imagine His Mother. One might say that every woman, every young girl, every young mother, every woman beholden to sorrow, every woman lonely and pensive—when she can rise above purely sensual or sentimental states— bears the image of a possible Mother of God. Thus the models of the Virgin are innumerable, and I daresay that there is no woman on earth who, in certain moments of joy or grief, of loving adoration, in the moments when she can remain simple without a loss of dignity, could not be a model for a Virgin Mary.

JEAN GUITTON

THE VIRGIN MOTHER

Mother! whose virgin bosom was uncrost
With the least shade of thought to sin allied;
Woman! Above all women glorified,
Our tainted nature's solitary boast;
Purer than foam on central ocean tost;
Brighter than eastern skies at daybreak strewn
With fancied roses, than the unblemished moon
Before her wane begins on heaven's blue coast;

Thy Image falls to earth. Yet some, I ween,
Not unforgiven the suppliant knee might bend,
As to a visible power, in which did blend
All that was mixed and reconciled in Thee
Of mother's love with maiden purity,
Of high with low, celestial with terrene!

WILLIAM WORDSWORTH

THE BLESSED MOTHER: AN IDEAL

That ideal love we see beyond all creature love, to which we instinctively turn when flesh-love fails, is the same ideal that God had in His Heart from all eternity—the Lady whom He calls ''Mother.'' She is the one whom every man loves when he loves a woman—whether he knows it or not. She is what every woman wants to be, when she looks at herself. She is the woman whom every man marries in ideal when he takes a spouse; she is hidden as an ideal in the discontent of every woman with the carnal aggressiveness of man; she is the secret desire every woman has to be honored and fostered; she is the way every woman wants to command respect and love because of the beauty of her goodness of body and soul. And this blueprint love, whom God loved before the world was made; this Dream Woman before women were, is the one of whom every heart can say in its depth of depths: ''She is the Woman I love!''

FJS

"BEHOLD THY MOTHER"

It may be objected: "Our Lord is enough for me, I have no need of (the Blessed Mother)." But *He* needed her, whether we do or not. And, what is more important, Our Blessed Lord gave us His Mother as *our* Mother. On that Friday men call Good, when He was unfurled upon the Cross as the banner of salvation, He looked down to the two most precious creatures He had on earth: His Mother and His beloved disciple, John. The night before, at the Last Supper, He had made His last Will and Testament giving us that which on dying no man was ever able to give, namely, Himself in the Holy Eucharist. Thus He would be with us, as He said: "All days unto the consummation of the world." Now in the darkening shadows of Calvary, He adds a codicil to His Will. There beneath the cross, not prostrate as the Gospel notes, "stood" His Mother. As a Son, He thought of His Mother; as a Saviour, He thought of us. So He gave to us His Mother: "Behold thy mother!"

FJS

The zone where two glad worlds forever meet
Beneath that bosom ;
Deep in that womb the conquering Paraclete
Smote Godhead onto man.

R. S. HAWKER

CHRIST
IN THE
UNIVERSE

*Our Lord called Himself the "Son of Man"
about eighty times, for it was the title of
humiliation and suffering. But He never used
the term after He had redeemed humanity
and had risen from the dead.*

FJS

THE LORD'S CREATION
Creation demands incarnation, which in turn finds its
consummation in the parousia of the Kingdom. Time is
built into the structure of the created world, which
means that the world is ''unfinished,'' ''embryonic,''
so as to further and direct that synergy of Divine power
and human power until the day of the Lord wherein the
seed attains its full fruition.
PAUL E. VODOKIMOV

PLANTING FOR CHRIST
If you are planting for a year,
      plant grain;
If you are planting for ten years,
      plant trees;
If you are planting for a hundred years,
      plant men.
CHINESE PROVERB

GOD'S OMNIPOTENT LOVE

What is love? Love is the power to grant freedom without desiring to limit or inhibit its exercise. It is the power to give freedom without any will to take it back. And it is only Omnipotence that can refrain absolutely from trespassing upon freedom. Only God can give and not take back. . . . He suffers within Himself the entire consequence of allowing man absolute freedom. That is His Love. . . .

Thus the existence of evil and suffering in the world is a proof, not that God is either Good but powerless, or All Powerful but not good. On the contrary, it is a proof that God is both loving and omnipotent. Only absolute love could grant unhindered freedom, and only omnipotence can endure the operation of that freedom.

D. R. DAVIES

CHRIST KNOWS YOUR NEEDS

I am moved with pity *for the multitude* : His compassion, because it was human, was spontaneous ; because it was Divine, was on the grand scale. We find our hearts go out in compassion towards this or that victim of poverty or distress, when a whole crowd of people is affected, our sympathy—our instinctive sympathy—grows fainter, just where it should have been redoubled ; if a whole sub-continent is ravaged by pestilence or famine, we put our hands in our pockets, but we are too unimaginative to feel the tragedy. With Our Lord, it is not so ; He has been dealing with them one by one, the blind, the dumb, the lame, the palsied and the possessed ; and now, contemplating them *en masse*, He is as conscious as ever of their common need. He has pity on the multitude.

RONALD KNOX

A LIFE LIVED BACKWARDS

Every other person but Christ came into this world to
live. He came into it to die. Death was a stumbling block
to Socrates—it interrupted his teaching. But to Christ,
death was the goal and fulfillment of His Life, the goal
that He was seeking. He was a Savior rather than a
teacher. The story of every human life begins with birth
and ends with death. In the Person of Christ, however, it
was His Death that was first and His Life that was last.
Scripture therefore describes Him as ''the Lamb slain as
it were, from the beginning of the world.'' It was not so
much His Birth that cast a shadow on His Life and thus
led to His Death; it was rather the Cross that was first
and cast a shadow back to His Birth. His has been the
only Life in the world that was ever lived backwards.

FJS

AT THE FEET OF CHRIST
Everyman ended up at the Feet of the Divine Son;
Plato's dreams move toward him . . .
Zeno's laws move toward him . . .
He became the heir of Latin prose.

CHARLES PÉGUY

LOVE UNLOVED
Ye call Me Master and obey Me not,
Ye call Me Light and see Me not,
Ye call Me Way and walk not,
Ye call Me Life and desire Me not,
Ye call Me Wise and follow Me not,
Ye call Me Fair and love Me not,
Ye call Me Rich and ask Me not,
Ye call Me Eternal and seek Me not,
Ye call Me Gracious and trust Me not,
Ye call Me Noble and serve Me not,
Ye call Me Mighty and honor Me not,
Ye call Me Just and fear Me not;
If I condemn you, blame Me not.

ENGRAVED ON THE CATHEDRAL OF LÜBECK, GERMANY

RULER OF THE UNIVERSE

With this ambiguous earth
His dealings have been told us. These abide :
The signal to a maid, the human birth,
The lesson, and the young man crucified.

But not a star of all
The innumerable hosts of stars has heard
How He administered this terrestrial ball.
Our race have kept their Lord's entrusted Word.
Of His earth-visiting Feet
None knows the secret, cherished, perilous,
The terrible, shamefast, frightened, whispered, sweet,
Heart-shattering secret of His way with us.

No planet knows that this
Our wayside planet, carrying land and wave,
Love and life multiplied, and pain and bliss,
Bears, as chief treasure one forsaken grave. . . .

O be prepared, my soul,
To read the inconceivable, to scan
The million forms of God, though stars unroll
When, in our turn, we show to them a Man.

ALICE MEYNELL

TO BE WITH CHRIST

I remembered a village priest in Provence who went
to the waiting room of the nearby railway junction every
night when most people were in bed, because there the
lonely gathered, men who had no home, men who could
not face home because of what they had done, men who
could not speak to any woman but a prostitute, men and
women who were failures because of their own fault or
someone else's fault or nobody's fault. He knew Christ
must be there; and he wished to be where Christ was, to
make visible to these people the Christ Whom they could
not see, to take their suffering and their sin upon him, as
Christ was, to pray for them, as Christ prayed.

J. W. STEVENSON

GIVE THE EARTH TO CHRIST

A little Boy of heavenly birth,
But far from home today,
Comes down to find His ball, the earth
That sin has cast away.
O comrades, let us one and all
Join in to get Him back His ball.

JOHN BANISTER TABB

UNSELFISH PRAYER

A young air commander who perished in the last World
War had this prayer in his pocket when he was found:

I send up my prayer to You, My God;
    For You can give what one cannot give himself.
Give me what no one ever asked for,
    I do not ask You for rest or peace, either of soul or body.
I do not ask you for wealth, success or even health,
    You are always being asked for all of this.
Give me, God, what you have left;
    I mean insecurity and anxiety: I mean torment and
        turmoil.
And I ask You to give them to me without fail,
    So that I am sure to have them always,
For I shall not always be brave enough to ask them always.
    Give me, my God, what You have left.
Give me what no one else wants.
    Give me also courage and strength and faith,
For You alone can give what one cannot give himself.

ANON

43

THE TRUE FATHERHOOD OF GOD

Love that desires to limit its own exercise is not love.
Love that is happier if it meets only one who needs help
rather than if it met ten—and happiest if it meets none
at all—is not love. One of love's essential laws is
expressed in the words of Our Lord that the Apostles
fondly remembered after He ascended: "It is more
blessed to give than to receive." Our nation will be
happier and our hearts will be gayer when we discover
the true brotherhood of man, but to do this we must
realize that we are a race of illegitimate children unless
there is also the Fatherhood of God.

FJS

RESISTING EVIL

Make no mistake about it : absolute non-resistance to evil
can only be sound and fruitful in the climate of Christian
sanctity—in other words, the only possible justification
for refusing to take up the sword is to be prepared to be
stretched out on the cross. . . . The false god changes
suffering into violence. The true God changes violence
into suffering.

GUSTAVE THIBON

Oh God, deliver me from this lust of always justifying
myself.

ST. AUGUSTINE

 44

HE GAVE NOT LIFE ALONE

Because he was a man
As well as He was God,
He loved His own goat-nibbled hills,
His crumbling Jewish sod
He bowed to Roman rule
And dared none to rebel
But oh the windflowers out of Naim,
We know He loved them well!
He must have loved its tongue,
His Aramaic brogue,
As much as any Norman loves
The accents of La Hogue
Discountried and diskinged
And watched from pole to pole,
A Jew at heart remains a Jew—
His nation is his soul.

. . . .

As heifers' to their young
Christ's bowels yearned to His sod—
He was the very Jew of Jews
And yet since He was God—
Oh you with frontiered hearts,
Conceive it if you can—
It was not life alone He gave
But country up for man.

EILEEN DUGGAN

45

THE WORD BECAME FLESH

The Jews in the wilderness had a tabernacle or tent
wherein they worshipped God, and there the glory of
God was seen, for over the tabernacle hovered the
Shekinah—the glorious light, the symbol of the Divine
Presence. This figure of the glory of God came to reality
in Christ, who is the brightness of the Father's glory,
the true Shekinah tabernacled amongst us. His flesh, that
is to say, His body of human nature was as a tabernacle
in which resided that Divine Nature of which the glory of
the Jewish tabernacle was the temple. Thus the tabernacle
of God was with men and He dwelt amongst us. That is
what John means when he said : ''The Word was made
flesh and dwelt amongst us.''

FJS

THE GIFT OF CALVARY

If we would see the incarnate Lord as He is in His reality,
we must recognize this fact : that there is in Him from
the beginning this inner direction towards a redemptive
death. Calvary is not just an historical accident. It is not
something which might not have happened if Pilate had
been a braver man or Judas a trustier man, or Caiaphas a
holier man. The circumstances might conceivably, might
perhaps very well, have been different : the upshot would
have been the same. In the tensions of His own Being,
there is an inner necessity for redeeming Death. ''The
wages of sin is death'' and Jesus comes to pay the wages
that men have so laboriously earned.

DOM GREGORY DIX

46

THE
SPIRIT

God cannot fill *you unless you empty yourself.*
God cannot enrich *you unless you impoverish yourself.*
God cannot exalt *you unless you humble yourself.*
FJS

THE SPIRIT AND BEAUTY

Question the beauty of the earth, the beauty of the sea,
the beauty of the wide air around you, the beauty of the
sky; question the order of the stars, the sun whose
brightness lights the day, the moon whose splendour
softens the gloom of the night; question the living
creatures that move in the waters, that roam upon the
earth, that fly through the air; the spirit that lies hidden,
the matter that is manifest; the visible things that are
ruled, the invisible that rule them; question all these.
They will all answer you: ''Behold and see, we are
beautiful.'' Their beauty is their confession of God. Who
made these beautiful changing things, if not one who is
beautiful and changeth not?

ST. AUGUSTINE

BELIEF

They alone are able truly to enjoy this world, who begin
with the world unseen. They alone enjoy it, who have
abstained from it. . . . They alone inherit it, who take it
as a shadow of the world to come, who for that world to
come relinquish it.

JOHN HENRY CARDINAL NEWMAN

IMMORTALITY OF THE SOUL

Poor Soul, the centre of my sinful earth,
Fenced by these rebel powers that thee array,
Why dost thou pine within and suffer dearth,
Painting thy outward walls so costly gay?
Why so large cost, having so short a lease,
Dost thou upon thy fading mansion spend?
Shall worms, inheritors of this excess,
Eat up thy charge? Is this thy body's end?
Then, Soul, live thou upon thy servant's loss,
And let that pine to aggravate thy store;
Buy terms divine in selling hours of dross;
Within be fed, without be rich no more:
So shalt thou feed on Death, that feeds on men,
And Death once dead, there's no more dying then!
WILLIAM SHAKESPEARE

SPIRIT FLOWN

How long it is since she with whom I lay,
Oh Lord, has left for thine my widowed bed;
Yet still our spirits mingle, as our clay,
And she half living yet, and I half dead.
VICTOR HUGO

SPIRIT OF DENIAL

Pain and suffering are from sin and selfishness, but sacrifice is not; it is from love. It is through want of love that pain arises. Suffering brings one to the door of the Temple; but love is the key that unlocks the door, and by transmuting pain into sacrifice prepares for the happiness of the everlasting dwellings.

Those who have themselves never felt hunger involuntarily through fasting, can little understand the legitimate demands of the poor, or the obligation to feed them in charity.

In like manner, those who never have experienced suffering, which can be a condition of love, cannot understand how Christian souls resign themselves to Someone Who first loved us.

FJS

MIRACLES IN THEIR TIME

Do not think that God will make thee just by a miracle.
If He wished a beautiful rose to grow in the stark cold of
winter He might do it well, but He doeth not such a
thing, for He deemeth it His will that it be done in true
order in May after the frost, by dew and many a rainfall
ordained and framed to accomplish it.

SUSO

MUSIC TO CHRIST

There is one harp that any hand can play,
And from its strings what harmonies arise!
There is one song that any mouth can say,—
A song that lingers when all singing dies.
When on their beads our Mother's children pray,
Immortal music charms the grateful skies.

JOYCE KILMER

THE SPIRIT OF CHRIST

We need a Christ today Who will make cords and drive buyers and sellers from our new temples; Who will blast the unfruitful fig tree; Who will talk of crosses and sacrifices and Whose voice will be like the voice of the raging sea. But He will not allow us to pick and choose among His words, discarding the hard ones and accepting the ones that please our fancy. We need a Christ Who will restore moral indignation, Who will make us hate evil with a passionate intensity, and love goodness to a point where we can drink death like water.

FJS

THE HOLY SPIRIT'S CALL

Homeless am I, O Lord: Whither shall I turn?
A wanderer in the desert, whither shall I turn?
I come to Thee at last, driven from every threshold;
And if Thy door be closed, whither shall I turn?

TAHIR—A PERSIAN MYSTIC

THE SPIRIT AND LOVE

As one that is possessed and burning with a fever loathes
and rejects the sweetest food or drink that you offer
him, because he burns with the fever and is vehemently
exercised by it, so those who burn with the heavenly,
sacred, solemn longing of the Spirit, and are smitten in
soul with love of the love of God, and are vehemently
exercised by the divine and heavenly fire which the Lord
came to send upon the earth, and desire that it should
speedily be kindled, and are aflame with the heavenly
longing for Christ. These consider all the glorious and
precious things of this age contemptible and hateful by
reason of the fire of the love of Christ, which holds
them fast and inflames them and burns them with a
Godward disposition. From which nothing of all that are
in heaven and earth and under the earth shall be able to
separate them, as the apostle Paul testified, saying:
"Who shall separate us from the love of Christ?"

ST. MACARIUS THE EGYPTIAN

ABSENCE OF THE SPIRIT

We would say that the Good Pagan is like the jealous
lover who has killed his beloved to keep her all his own.
He holds her body cold and inanimate. He is the master of
the lifeless thing, but all that made her what she was, is
gone. He holds an empty likeness in his arms and even
soon that will perish and putrefy.

ROSALIND MURRAY

SIN

Sin, in all its forms, is the deliberate eviction
of Love from the soul. Sin is the enforced absence
of Divinity.
FJS

THE SINNER'S WAY

These are several ways to avoid loving God: Deny that
you are a sinner. Pretend that religion is for the ignorant
and the superstitious, but not for the truly learned such
as yourself. Insist that the sole purpose of religion is
social service. Judge religion by whether or not it is
accepted by the "important" people of the world. Avoid
all contemplation, self-examination and inquiry into the
moral state of your soul. Take yourself very seriously.

FJS

THE DECEIVING ANTICHRISTS

The thing that starts the quarrel between spirit and life
—the two entities that divide human life between them—
is what is at once most universal and most central. Its
ramifications can be seen in countless sub-conflicts, for
every part of man, every aspect, can become an idol.
Without leaving our own age we have examples in the
"sexual man of Freud" and the "political man of
Mussolini" and the "race man of Hitler" and the
"economic man of Marx"—each an idolatrous and
bloated enlargement of one side of man, and each in
conflict with the rest that it seeks to obliterate or absorb.
And the conflicts are unappeasable, because the
antagonists are not human realities: they are substitutes
for God—in other words they are idols.

GUSTAVE THIBON

SIN'S PUNISHMENT

When, instead of making a loving return to this fiery
dart of love, the soul sets up a final resistance, can there
be a better statement of the facts than to describe the
result as a punishment of fire? If even the mystic feels a
pain for which there is no true word, save that of fire,
the resistant soul already chafed by loss and schism
within must be blown into a living furnace by the wind of
Divine Love. Hell is the everlasting funeral pyre of Love.

M. C. D'ARCY

THOUGHT AS SIN

Our Lord went into the soul and laid hold of a thought,
and branded even the desire for sin as sin. If it was
wrong to do a certain thing, it was wrong to think about
that thing. He would say ''away with your hygiene
which strives to keep hands clean after they have stolen,
and bodies free from disease after they have ravished
another.'' He went into the depths of the heart and
branded even the intention to do evil as evil. He did not
wait for the evil tree to bear evil fruit. He would prevent
the very sowing of the evil seed. He would wait not until
hidden sins come out as psychoses and neuroses and
compulsions. He suggested getting rid of them at their
sources. Repent! Purge! Evil that can be put into
statistics, or that can be locked in jails, is almost too
late to remedy.

FJS

THE ROOTS OF SIN

When men and women reach a point where they are no longer interested in watching a seed that they have planted grow, or caring for its flower; when they are more concerned about increasing dollars in their bank account than obeying the primitive impulse to increase and multiply—then know ye that a night has dawned when a *thing* is more important than a *person,* and *Hic jacet* must be inscribed on the tombstone of democracy. Beyond and behind all the schemes and blueprints of politics and economics, there is nothing more fundamental to the revival of true democracy than the restoration of the family. In that circle shall our citizens learn that there is other wealth than paper wealth, paper money, paper stocks, paper joys, namely, the tingling, vibrating wealth of children, the unbreakable bond between husband and wife, the pledge of democracy and the future heirs of the Kingdom of Heaven.

FJS

Men are in their essential personality irreducibly diverse; but sin blots out the distinction and reduces the diversity.

F. J. SHEED

HATE'S AWFUL DUNGEON

I wonder if we ought not to think of Hell, more than we
do, in connection with our ordinary, dreary, Saturday
after Saturday sins? Not that they deserve Hell; oh no,
they are venial sins all right. But the point of Hell is not
simply that it is a punishment of our sins; it is also, in
a sense, the continuation of our sins; what really makes
Hell so unpleasant is what makes our sins so unpleasant
—the setting up of wrong standards, the clinging to
oneself and one's own point of view, the want of
submissiveness, the want of peace, the want of love. Going
to Hell is going to a place where all the people, not just
some people, all the time, not just some of the time, are
trying to assert themselves and hating one another.
RONALD KNOX

YOUR KIND OF HELL

Suppose you hated mathematics and you had to live in
the companionship of mathematicians. Suppose the
morning paper was filled with nothing but logarithms,
and every conversation of the day was on mathematical
physics, and every book on your shelf was a treatise on
calculus. Would not mathematics be your hell?
FJS

THE DESTRUCTIVE SPIRIT

I am really split in two mentally, and I am horribly
afraid of it. It is just as though one's second self was
standing beside one; one is sensible and rational, but
the other self is impelled to do something perfectly
senseless, and something very funny; and suddenly you
notice that you are longing to do that amusing thing,
goodness knows why; that is you want to, as it were,
against your will; though you fight against it with all
your might, you want to. . . . do you know here I have
taken up the icon again (he had picked it up and was
turning it about in his hand), and do you know, I have a
dreadful longing now this very second to smash it against
the stove, against this corner. I am sure it would break
into two halves—neither more nor less. (And the image
broke into two pieces exactly.)

DOSTOEVSKI

FRUITS OF SIN

Each sinner kindles for himself the flame of his own fire.
. . . The fuel of this fire is our sins, which feed it. It
seems to me that just as too much food or its bad quality
produces fevers in the body, so the soul heaps up
sins and misdeeds, and in due course this accumulation
of wickedness catches fire in retribution and flares up as
punishment.

ORIGEN

SIN IN ACTION

Let Him come into a world which tries to interpret man
in terms of sex; which regards purity as coldness;
chastity as frustrated sex; self-containment as
abnormality; and the union of husband and wife
until death as a boredom; which says that a marriage
only endures so long as the glands thrill, and that one
may unbind what God binds and unseal what God seals.
Let Him say to them "Blessed are the pure of heart"
and He will find Himself hanging naked on a cross, made
a spectacle to men and angels in a last, wild, crazy
affirmation that purity is abnormal, that virgins are
neurotic, and that sexuality is right.

FJS

"We have our hell on earth," some say. Right! But it
does not end here. We just ignite it here.

FJS

REFUSAL TO LOVE

Love can forgive injuries, betrayals and insults, and
Divine Love can forgive even to seventy times seven. But
there is only one thing in the world which human love
cannot forgive, and there is only one thing in eternity
which Divine Love cannot forgive and that is the refusal
to love, because that makes forgiveness impossible. Hell
is the place where there is no love.

FJS

 61

THE NEVER-SATISFIED

Saint Catherine of Genoa, in the course of one of her
visions, argues with God about Hell; she is absolutely
certain that the sinner will be better off if entrusted to
her love. God gives her *carte blanche* and Catherine
hastens to seize a thoroughly hardened sinner whom she
pushes, and drives, and shoves, willy-nilly, into the very
centre of Paradise, into the very heart of God, into the
splendour of all light. Whereupon the soul thus com-
mandeered into Paradise is violently angered, and
protests: ''Why, O God, didst thou deliver me over to
this sentimental and foolish woman; what is my crime
that now I must suffer a punishment which is spared even
the Devil; no suffering in Hell could match the torture of
being drowned in love when everything within me is
corrupt.'' Catherine, undismayed and thinking, no
doubt, that with a little practice she will learn to handle
souls, takes the sinner and places him outside of Paradise
but also outside of Hell. A rending cry rises to God:
'' And now I am nowhere, now I am truly *lost*. I beg that
I may be allowed to reenter Hell where, through divine
justice, I still form part of order. Thy justice, O God,
which is a presence, lightens a little the terrible verdict
of damnation; thine absence, thy punishment bring a
little order into chaos—into negative and eternal
absurdity.''

ST. CATHERINE OF GENOA

EVIL'S EVENTUAL FAILURE

Evil will never be stronger than it was on Good Friday.
The worst thing that evil can do is not to bomb cities and
kill children and to wage wars; the worst thing that
evil can do is to kill Goodness. Having been defeated in
that, it could never be victorious again.

Goodness in the face of evil must suffer, for when Love
meets sin, it will be crucified. A God Who wears His
Sacred Heart upon His sleeve, as Our Lord did when He
became Man, must be prepared to have daws peck at it.
But evil conquered in its full armor and in a moment of
its monumental momentum, will in the future win some
battles, but it will never win the war.

FJS

REFUGE OF SINNERS

It is so easy to lose Christ; He can even be lost by a little
heedlessness; a little want of watchfulness and the Divine
Presence slips away. But sometimes a reconciliation is
sweeter than an unbroken friendship. There are two
ways of knowing how good God is: one is never to lose
Him, the other is to lose Him and find Him again. Sin is
the loss of Jesus, and since Mary felt the sting of His
absence she could understand the gnawing heart of every
sinner and be to it, in the truest sense of the word:
"Refuge of Sinners."

FJS

 63

THE ROAD TO HELL

Consider your wrist watch. It has wheels. Suppose every wheel were self-conscious and wanted to be independent. And suppose one of the wheels said "I am tired of being kicked in the teeth! I will be independent. I will unhook myself from my environment and be *me*. I will turn when I choose and I will refuse to turn when someone kicks me around!"... It no longer tells time nor serves man.

God has allowed us independence if we want it. Lots of people do want it, and they get it. But what do they get with it? Selfishness and egocentricity. And selfishness leads to corrosion of personality because it isolates. And isolation is the road to hell.

KENNETH L. PIKE

VICTORY OVER DEATH

In the death of Lazarus, Our Lord saw that long procession of mourners from the first to the last, and the reason of it all: sin, whose penalties He would assume and give death its death.

FJS

AS YOU SOW, YOU REAP

Hell is not related to an evil life as spanking is related
to an act of disobedience, for a spanking need not follow
the breaking of a law. Rather hell is related to an evil life
in the same way that blindness is related to the plucking
out of an eye, for the two are inseparable. Life is a
harvest and we reap what we sow : if we sow in sin we
reap corruption ; if we sow in the spirit, we reap life
everlasting.

FJS

DISOBEDIENCE

Within the infant rind of this small flower
    Poison hath residence and medicine power :
For this, being smelt, with that part cheers each part ;
    Being tasted, slays all senses with the heart.
Two such opposed kings encamp them still
    In man as well as herbs, grace and rude will.

WILLIAM SHAKESPEARE

The doors of hell are locked from the inside.

FJS

CHRIST

Seven times the night before our Lord died, He told His disciples that they would be hated by the world. When we get on too well with the world, there must be something wrong with us.
FJS

THE SUFFERING CHRIST

If He was to suffer, He gave Himself to suffering; He
did not come to suffer as little as He could; He did not
turn away His Face from the suffering: He confronted
it, or, as I may say, He breasted it, that every particular
portion of it might make its due impression on Him. And
as men are superior to brute animals, and are affected by
pain more than they, by reason of the mind within them,
which gives them a substance to pain such as it cannot
have in the instance of brutes; so in like manner, Our
Lord felt pain of the body with an advertence and a
consciousness, and therefore, with a keenness and
intensity, and with a unity of perception, none of us
can possibly fathom or compass, because His Soul was
so absolutely in His own power, so simply free from the
influence of distractions, so fully directed upon the pain,
so utterly surrendered, so utterly subjected to the
suffering. And thus He may truly be said to have suffered
the whole of His Passion in every moment of it.

JOHN HENRY CARDINAL NEWMAN

A SMILE IN HIS HEART

A man on earth He wandered once,
All meek and undefiled,
And those who loved Him said "He wept"—
None ever said "He smiled";
Yet there might have been a smile unseen,
When He bowed His Holy Face, I ween
To bless that happy child.

ELIZABETH BARRETT BROWNING

GOD'S REVELATION

When God revealed Himself, when God wished to show
what He was really like, He revealed that He was love,
tenderness, a fusion of Himself, infinite kindness towards
others, affection, subordination. God revealed Himself
to be obedient, obedient unto death. Whilst believing that
he was becoming God, Adam became totally different
from Him. He entrenched himself in solitude, and God
was but communion.

L. EVELY

SEEK CHRIST

It was not right that Jesus Christ should appear in a
manner which was Divine and absolutely capable of
convincing all men ; but neither was it right that He
should come in a manner so hidden that He could not be
known by those who sought Him sincerely. He wanted to
make Himself perfectly recognizable to these. And so,
willing to appear plainly to those who sought Him with
all their heart, He shades His knowledge, so as to give
visible signs of Himself to those who sought Him and not
to those who sought Him not. There is light enough for
those who only desire to see, and obscurity enough for
those whose disposition is otherwise.

PASCAL, *Pensées*

IN-CHRISTED

Christ be with me, Christ within me,
Christ behind me, Christ before me,
Christ beside me, Christ to win me,
Christ to comfort and restore me,
Christ beneath me, Christ above me,
Christ in quiet, Christ in danger,
Christ in hearts of all that love me,
Christ in mouth of friend and stranger.

ST. PATRICK

THE GIVER OF LIFE

My heart is weak and poor
　　Until it master find;
It has no spring of action sure—
　　It varies with the wind:
It cannot freely move
　　Till Thou hast wrought its chain;
Enslave it with Thy matchless love
　　And deathless it shall reign.

. . . .

My will is not my own
　　Till Thou hast made it Thine;
If it would reach a monarch's throne
　　It must its crown resign:
It only stands unbent
　　Amid the clashing strife,
When on Thy bosom it has leant,
　　And found in Thee its life.

GEORGE MATHESON

WHEN CHRIST SANG

The only recorded time in the history of Our Lord that
He ever sang was the night He went out to the Garden
of Gethsemane and His Death.

FJS

 71

CHRIST'S MATCHLESS LOVE

Love the Revealer—are you prepared for that? For
seeing of what God truly is, and of what you are?
Love the Purifier—and how shall this be without pain?
Love the Illuminator—can you bear the Light?
Love the All-Demanding—are you willing to be an
abandoned lover?
Love the Forgiver—but have you forgiven?
Love the Perfecter—but
   Many a blow and biting sculpture
   Polished well those stones elect.
Love the Peace-Bringer—but who brings
   a sword, for peace may reign only when the war with
   self within and evil without has been fought and won.
BEDE FROST, O.S.B.

LIFE'S INCOMPLETENESS

I say to the seventy-five per cent of Hindus receiving
instruction in this college, that your lives also will
be incomplete unless you reverently study the teachings
of Jesus.
GANDHI

CONDEMNED FOR "YOUR" SIN

Why did not Our Lord condemn the woman taken in sin?
Because He would be condemned for her. Innocence does
not condemn when Innocence suffers for the guilty.
FJS

 72

THE ANTICHRIST

The Antichrist appears as an emperor and addresses Christians but will not pronounce the Divine Name of Jesus Christ.

In a grieved voice the emperor addressed them : ''What else can I do for you, you strange people? What do you want from me? I cannot understand. Tell me yourselves, you Christians, deserted by the majority of your brothers and leaders, condemned by popular sentiment : What is it you value most in Christianity?''

At this Elder John rose, like a white candle, and said in a quiet voice : ''Great sovereign, the thing we value most in Christianity is Christ Himself—He in His Person. All the rest cometh from Him. For we know that in Him dwelleth bodily the fullness of Divinity. But we are ready, Sire, to accept any gift from you as well, if only we recognize the holy Hand of Christ in your generosity. Our candid answer to your question, what can you do for us, is this : Here now and before us, name the Name of Jesus Christ, the Son of God Who came into the flesh, rose and is coming again—name His Name, and we will accept you with love as the true forerunner of His Second glorious Coming.''

But the emperor could not pronounce the Holy Name since He was Antichrist.

VLADIMIR SOLOVIEV

 73

JESUS ALONE

Two verses in the Gospel of John should not be separated :
the last verse of chapter seven and the first verse of
chapter eight.

And they went back, each to his own home (John 7:53).
Jesus meanwhile, went to the Mount of Olives (John 8:1).

FJS

CHRIST AT CALVARY

I saw the Son of God go by
   Crowned with a crown of Thorn.
"Was it not finished, Lord?" I said,
   "And all the anguish borne?"

He turned on me His awful eyes :
   "Hast thou not understood?
Lo! Every soul is Calvary
   And every sin a Rood."

RACHEL ANNAND TAYLOR

74

THE ABUSED SAVIOR

It is clear that Christ did not find His inner peace from
His environment. As a Baby in His Mother's arms no
doubt He had the security which is every babe's
birthright. . . . When He called His twelve Apostles to be
with Him, they were not nice, quiet people with whom it
is easy to live. Two of them, who sound to us gentle
enough, were called ''the Sons of Thunder.'' They all
seemed to have quarreled for precedence. They all
misunderstood Christ's purposes, and they all forsook
Him when He needed them most. He died almost alone,
His cause apparently defeated, His followers scattered,
His Body tortured, His Mind just before His Death in
the agony of what felt like desertion. Yet perhaps in His
last words He gave us a lifetime secret : ''Father, into
Thy Hands I commend My Spirit !''

LESLIE D. WEATHERHEAD

JESUS OF THE SCARS

If we have never sought, we seek Thee now;
 Thine eyes burn through the dark, our only stars;
We must have sight of thorn-pricks on Thy brow,
 We must have Thee, O Jesus of the Scars.

The heavens frighten us; they are too calm;
 In all the universe we have no place.
Our wounds are hurting us; where is the balm?
 Lord Jesus, by Thy Scars we claim Thy grace.

If when the doors are shut, Thou drawest near,
 Only reveal those hands, that side of Thine;
We know to-day what wounds are, have no fear,
 Show us Thy Scars, we know the countersign.

The other gods were strong; but Thou wast weak;
 They rode, but Thou didst stumble to a throne;
But to our wounds only God's wounds can speak,
 And not a god has wounds, but Thou alone.

EDWARD SHILLITO

A NEW YOU IN CHRIST

The Christian way is different, harder, and easier. Christ says: "Give me All. I do not want so much of your time, and so much of your money, and so much of your work: I want You. I have not come to torment your natural self, but to kill it. No half measures are any good. I do not want to cut off a branch here and a branch there, I want to have the whole tree cut down. I do not want to drill a tooth, or crown it, or stop it, but to have it out. Hand over the whole natural self, all the desires which you think innocent as well as the ones you think wicked—the whole outfit, and I will give you a new self instead. In fact, I will give you Myself: My own Will shall become yours."

C. S. LEWIS

LOVE THAT MAKES SAINTS

*The night of the Last Supper the Apostles were
quarreling as to who would have the first place
at table among themselves. Our Blessed Lord
then got down on His knees, washed their feet
and wiped them with a towel.* How few there are
who ever fight for the towel.

FJS

THE KINGDOM OF GOD

O World invisible, we view thee,
O world intangible, we touch thee,
O world unknowable, we know thee,

Inapprehensible, we clutch thee!
Does the fish soar to find the ocean,
The eagle plunge to find the air—
That we ask of the stars in motion
If they have rumour of thee there?

Not where the wheeling systems darken,
And our benumbed conceiving soars!—
The drift of pinions, would we hearken,
Beats at our own clay-shuttered doors.

The angels keep their ancient places;—
Turn but a stone and start a wing!
'Tis ye, 'tis your estrangèd faces,
That miss the many-splendoured thing.

But (when so sad thou canst not sadder)
Cry;—and upon thy so sore loss
Shall shine the traffic of Jacob's ladder
Pitched betwixt Heaven and Charing Cross.

Yea, in the night, my Soul, my daughter,
Cry,—clinging Heaven by the hems;
And lo, Christ walking on the water
Not of Gennesareth, but Thames!

FRANCIS THOMPSON

STRIVING TOWARD SAINTHOOD

Let us never deceive youth by foolish talk about the matter of accomplishing. Let us never make them busy in the service of the moment, instead of in patience willing something eternal. Let us not make them quick to judge what they perhaps do not understand, instead of willing something eternal and being content with little for themselves.

SØREN KIERKEGAARD

BLESSED GIVER

Love ever gives—
Forgives, outlives—
And ever stands
With open hands,
And while it lives
It gives
For this is Love's prerogative
To give—and give—and give.

JOHN OXENHAM

GOD'S LAW

I remember my mother warned me in private not to commit fornication, and especially not to defile another man's wife. These seemed to me womanish advices, which I should blush to obey. But they were Thine, O God, and I knew it not.

ST. AUGUSTINE

 81

THE ROAD TO GOD

The man who constantly keeps in his heart the *one*
concern not to lose contact with the Hand of God, will be
able to allow a sovereign carefreeness, to govern
everything with which he is then in duty bound to
concern himself, simply because he is prepared at any
time to let God cancel and throw away his own plans
and programs. For he knows that the Father's red pencil
is not the terrifying instrument of an evil and
incalculable censor, but rather that this is the only way
that God can lead us to His royal goal. He knows
therefore that every red check is not only a sign of
judgment, but rather a sign of grace, erected above our
shortsighted and deluded eyes, and assurance that He
is at work and that He will not allow us to fall victim
to our well-meant follies and plans.

HELMUT THIELICKE

THE SOURCE OF ALL TRUTH

When a man rests his weight upon the beautiful goods of
sight and sense his "happiness" fluctuates with every
change of circumstance. Anxiety is the inner dread of
this unsteady support. . . . Our feeling of groundlessness
(and the dread of it) is meant to prod us toward the
truth—that God alone is our true ground and end.

SEWARD HILTNER *and* KARL MENNINGER

All that is essential for the triumph of evil is that good
men do nothing.

EDMUND BURKE

 82

FROM MAN TO SAINT

The transition from the good man to the saint is a sort of
revolution; by which one for whom all things illustrate
and illuminate God becomes one for whom God illustrates
and illuminates all things. It is rather like the reversal
whereby a lover might say at first sight that a lady looked
like a flower, and say afterward that all flowers
reminded him of his lady. A saint and a poet standing
by the same flower might seem to say the same thing; but
indeed though they would both be telling the truth, they
would be telling different truths. For one the joy of life
is a cause of faith, for the other a result of faith. . . . The
mystic who passes through the moment when there is
nothing but God does in some sense behold the
beginningless beginnings in which there was really
nothing else. He not only appreciates everything, but the
nothing of which everything was made. In a fashion he
endures and answers even the earthquake irony of the
book of Job; in some sense he is there when the
foundations of the world are laid, with the morning stars
singing together and the sons of God shouting for joy.

ST. FRANCIS OF ASSISI

PENANCE

Wouldst thou learn that the penalty He is
exacting of thee is less, far less,
than thy sins deserve.

JOB 11 :6

 83

GOD'S THERAPY

God's grace is God's therapy for man's *primal* anxiety.
... In an atmosphere of acute anxiety, a person will
"decode" the anxiety signals that he perceives quite
differently from the one who feels upborne, accepted and
beloved. Grace displaces one "atmosphere" (anxiety)
with another "atmosphere" (buoyance).

SEWARD HILTNER *and* KARL MENNINGER

THE ETERNAL IN MAN

The indolent youth speaks of a long life that lies before
him. The indolent old man hopes that his death is still a
long way off. But repentance and remorse belong to the
eternal in a man.

SØREN KIERKEGAARD

Of courtesy, it is much less
Than courage of heart or holiness,
Yet in my walks it seems to me
That the grace of God is in courtesy.

HILAIRE BELLOC

GOD BUILDS HUMAN TEMPLES

Imagine yourself as a living house. God comes in to rebuild that house. At first, perhaps, you can understand what He is doing. He is getting the drains right and stopping the leaks in the roof and so on : you knew that those jobs needed doing and so you are not surprised. But presently He starts knocking the house about in a way that hurts abominably and does not seem to make sense. What on earth is He up to? The explanation is that He is building quite a different house from the one you thought of—throwing out a new wing here, putting on an extra floor there, running up towers, making courtyards. You thought you were going to be made into a decent little cottage : but He is building a palace. He intends to come and live in it Himself.

C. S. LEWIS

God has His best gifts for the few who dare to stand the test. His second choice He has for those who will not have His best.

ANON

TO SEE OTHERS

The man whose heart was hardened by wealth went to Rabbi Eisig. The Rabbi said to him: "Look out of the window, and tell me what you see in the street." "I see people walking up and down." Then he gave him a looking glass: "Look in this and tell me what you see." The man replied: "I see myself." "So you do not see others anymore? Consider that the window and the mirror are both made of glass; but, since the mirror has a coating of silver, you only see yourself in it, while you can see others through the transparent glass of the window. I am very sorry to have to compare you to these two kinds of glass. When you were poor, you saw others and had compassion on them; but being covered with wealth, you see only yourself. It would be much the best thing for you to scrape off the silver coating so that you can again see other people."

JEAN DE MENASCE

I have not done what God desired of me; that is certain. On the contrary, I have only dreamed of what I wanted from God.

LÉON BLOY

TO SAVE MYSELF

Sunder me from my soul, that I may see
The sins like streaming wounds, the life's brave beat;
'Til I shall save myself, as I would save
A stranger in the street.

G. K. CHESTERTON

 86

TRUE DENIAL

In order to have pleasure in everything
Desire to have pleasure in nothing.
In order to arrive at possessing everything
Desire to possess nothing.
In order to arrive at being everything
Desire to be nothing.
In order to arrive at knowing everything
Desire to know nothing.
In order to arrive at that wherein thou hast no pleasure
Thou must go by a way in which thou hast no pleasure.
In order to arrive at that which thou knowest not
Thou must go by a way that thou knowest not.
In order to arrive at that which thou possessest not
Thou must go by a way that thou possessest not.
In order to arrive at that which thou art not
Thou must go through that which thou art not.

ST. JOHN OF THE CROSS

CORRECT ORDER

God first
Others next
Self last

ANON

AS LITTLE CHILDREN

No old people ever enter the Kingdom of Heaven:
"Unless you become as little children, you shall not
enter the Kingdom of Heaven." MATTHEW 18:3

FJS

 87

AUTHORITY AS A SERVICE

The Savior dreamed of establishing within His Church a regime of humility and love. Was it not for this reason that He chose for the first representative of supreme authority in the Church, for the first Pope, a man of no importance, who could not bring himself into the argument; a fisherman, who was likewise a sinner; a penitent who made a triple act of love that was sealed by martyrdom? And thus to prove at the same time that authority is not a fief, but a service, and since it is a service, it is the proper office of love, even if it be love unto death.

A. G. SERTILLANGES

The saints are the sinners who keep on trying.
ROBERT LOUIS STEVENSON

GOD IS ALL-SUFFICIENT

Let nothing disturb thee,
Nothing affright thee;
All things are passing;
God never changeth;
Patient endurance
Attaineth to all things;
Who God possesseth
In nothing is wanting;
Alone God sufficeth.

ST. TERESA OF AVILA

TO TRANSFORM OTHERS

The world that you want to transform in a just manner
will not be transformed because you yourselves are not
transformed. And so long as you refuse to change
yourselves, the world will not change. But the world can
change if you change. How do you change? By listening
to God, because as the sun is always shining, God is
constantly speaking.

PÈRE GRATARY

THE VETERAN

When I was young and strong and bold,
Oh, right was right, and wrong was wrong!
My plume on high, my flag unfurled,
I rode away to right the world.
"Come out, you dogs, and fight!" said I,
And wept there was but once to die.

But I am old; and good and bad
Are woven in a crazy plaid.
I sit and say, "The world is so;
and he is wise who lets it go.
A battle lost, a battle won—
The difference is small, my son."

Inertia rides and riddles me;
The which is called philosophy.

DOROTHY PARKER

 89

TREASURES OF THE SAINTS

When we are members of the Mystical Body, we have at
our disposal, for loving, understanding and serving God
not only our own powers but everything from the Blessed
Virgin in the summit of Heaven down to the poor African
leper who, bell in hand, whispers the responses of the
Mass through a mouth half-eaten away. The whole of
creation, visible and invisible, all history, all the past,
and the present and the future, all the treasures of the
saints multiplied by grace—all that is at our disposal as
an extension of ourselves, a mighty instrument. All the
saints and angels belong to us. We can use the
intelligence of St. Thomas or the right arm of St.
Michael, the hearts of Joan of Arc and Catherine of
Siena, and all the hidden resources which have only to be
touched to be set in action. Everything of the good, the
great and the beautiful, from one end of the earth to the
other—everything which begets sanctity (as a doctor says
of a patient that he has *got* a fever)—it is as if all that
were our work. The heroism of the missionary, the
inspiration of the Doctors of the Church, the generosity
of the martyrs, the genius of the artists, the burning
prayers of the Poor Clares and Carmelites—it is as if all
that were ourselves; it is ourself.

PAUL CLAUDEL

A man would do nothing, if he waited until he could do
it so well that no one at all would find fault with what
he has done.

JOHN HENRY CARDINAL NEWMAN

 90

THE
CHURCH

Let us see the Church as Mother to be loved. If papal primacy were presented to us as meaning first in service, and as the response to the threefold question of love Christ put to Peter, it would be a language that all Christians, even non-Christians, understood.

FJS

MEMBERS OF CHRIST'S BODY

And so the passion of Christ is not in Christ alone; and yet the passion of Christ is in Christ alone. For if in Christ you consider both the Head and the body, then Christ's passion is in Christ alone; but if by Christ you mean only the Head, then Christ's passion is not in Christ alone.... Hence if you are in the members of Christ whatever you suffer at the hands of those who are not among the members of Christ, was lacking to the sufferings of Christ. It is added precisely because it was lacking. You fill up the measure, you do not cause it to overflow. You will suffer just so much as must be added of your sufferings to the complete Passion of Christ, who suffered as our Head and who continues still to suffer in His members, that is, in us. Into this common treasury each pays what he owes, and according to each one's ability we all contribute our share of suffering. The full measure of the Passion will not be attained until the end of the world.

ST. AUGUSTINE

THE HOUSE OF GOD

To come into the Church is not to cut oneself off from the
"others." To have a home of one's own can lead to
selfish exclusiveness; but it also can enable us to welcome
and offer a home to others, helping them to draw nearer
to God "in the house of the Father here below." If I may
put it so the "others" are separated from Christ only by
a door that is always open.

J. M. PERRIN

PRAISE IN SONGS

I am a swallow that could not find its way home in the
    Autumn, but your voice is like the rush of wings. . . .
You lift your head to Heaven and the crown of it is not
    singed.
  You stride to the borders of hell and your feet are
    unhurt.
You profess eternity and your soul is unafraid.
  You order certainty and your lips are not silenced.

GERTRUDE VON LE FORT

93

PRAYER IN HIS CHURCH

When we are young, in the full vigor of love, the prayer
of the body is a thing of delight, like a spontaneous cry
of joy to God. It is full of the sweetness of living, of the
potentiality of pure love, of responses to the sun and light
and darkness, as vibrant and mysterious and sweet as
those of the seed in the earth or the sap in the tree. Our
strength, our sense of well-being, is something like a
shout of praise to God, our five senses like five angels
bring us the messages of His Love with touches and
tongues of fire. . . .

As time passes, when we get older, or if we fall ill, or even
more if we gather to ourselves the little crop of ailments
that are part of the fair wear-and-tear of life, we require
more discipline, and of a different kind. . . . It is
time to think about the part which the body has taken in
Christ's prayer in His Church for the last two thousand
years: I mean the liturgy. . . . It is not subject, as our
personal prayer is, to moods. It never fails . . . At the same
time it is the chorus of the whole human race made one in
communion with Christ.

CARYLL HOUSELANDER

PROCLAIMING CHRIST EFFECTIVELY

Because only ten per cent of the population are regular worshipers, does the fault lie with the faith of the Church? This would seem from the Gospels to be quite a gratuitous assumption. Indeed it may very well be that if Christ were proclaimed more effectively, the churches might be emptier still. As Dean Inge observed, the big battalions are not drawn up outside the narrow way. The customer is always right may be a good business slogan but it is quite fatal to the Church. The basic problem of communications is not *how* we put things but what we put. May it not be that it is our popularity rather than our unpopularity that should worry us? The Gospels are full of the theme that servants must not expect to get better treatment than their master—and the Master was rejected and crucified.

O. FIELDING CLARKE

GENERATING BELIEVERS

As the whole human race was born from Adam and his wife, so from Christ and His Church the whole multitude of believers has been generated.

ST. JEROME

THE LIVING GOSPEL

Christ lived a physical life two thousand years ago in a
human body taken from Mary ; so now He lives a mystical
life in a body drawn from the womb of humanity. The
written Gospel is the record of His historical life. The
Church is the living Gospel and record of His present life.

We do not become Christians by going back nineteen
hundred years and studying the life of Christ and
imitating His example, and then concluding we should
venerate this great Personage. The Christian, rather, is
born in the womb of a religious, corporate society just
as a citizen is born in the womb of a political society. He
lives by it, before he knows it, before he judges it, before
he seeks its sources, before he knows its tradition. He
creates him spiritually by baptism of the spirit, as his
fatherland creates him by the birth of his flesh. The
Church is that without which Christ would be limited
and imperfect. If we do not see Him living today in His
Mystical Body we would not have seen Him living
nineteen hundred years ago in His physical body. If we
do not believe the Mystical Body to be Divine, because it
is also so human, then we would not have believed the
physical body to be Divine, because it was crucified. If
we miss the Lord Jesus it is not because He is too far
away—it is because He is too close.

FJS

 96

FOR CHRIST OR COUNTRY

Today a movement which has grown up outside the
Catholic hierarchy is urging us on to attack him who
represents the Pope, who represents Jesus Christ. . . .
Gentlemen, I have only one soul and I cannot divide it
up ; but I have a body which can be divided up. It seems
to me the best thing to do is to offer my whole soul to God
and the Holy Church, and my body to my country. . . .
Since I cannot remedy the conflict in which the Church
and State are opposed, there is nothing I can offer up
better than to offer my soul to one side and my body to
the other, and sacrifice, in the hope of promoting
understanding between them. . . . I am a Chinese
Catholic. I love my country ; I also love my Church. I
dissociate myself from everything that is opposed to the
laws of my country, just as I dissociate myself from
everything which is opposed to the laws of my Church,
and above all things I dissociate myself from everything
which can sow discord. But if the Church and the
government cannot come to an agreement, sooner or
later, every Chinese Catholic will have nothing left to do
but die. Then why should one not offer one's body at once
to hasten the mutual understanding of all the parties
concerned.

FATHER TONG CHE-TCHE

THE CHURCH AND POVERTY

The Church must find again an aspect that has become a
little blurred through the centuries: the look of poverty.
Remembering that the Apostles were no more than
humble Galilean fishermen and that the Lord Himself
was pleased to live in poverty, the Church will strive to
be more completely faithful to this ideal.

CARDINAL LIÉNART

CHURCH AND RELIGION

Personal encounter of any kind can be terrifying. That is
why people want to depersonalize God's love and play it
cool. Otherwise it is felt to be too threatening. The
conventions of polite society, social etiquette, and so
forth, are a device to protect people from the onslaught
of personal encounter. . . . I think that quite a lot of
religious programs and rules we adopt are parallel to
social etiquette. They help us not to meet the personal,
common, human charity of God. We escape from the real
world, where we meet God's charity, and what we are
and what other people are, escape into an alternative,
less threatening world called religion and church.

H. A. WILLIAMS

THE GLORY OF THE CHURCH

Everywhere where I have recalled in these books that the
Church has neither spot nor wrinkle, this must not be
taken in the sense that she is already thus, but rather, that
she is in preparation to become such when she appears in
glory. Now, in fact, because of the ignorance and
feebleness of her members, she may as a whole
say everyday, ''Forgive us our trespasses.''
ST. AUGUSTINE

LIFE FOR YOUR SOUL

One of the Gospel values is the supremacy of love over
legalism. Too much emphasis on legalism, the result
of seeing the Church above all as a society, risks making
obedience of the faithful to the ''laws'' of the Church
into something purely external, passive and material.
People go to Mass on Sunday because the ''laws'' of the
Church require it. They do not know why the Church
requires it. They do not know that the Church requires it
so that their souls may receive life. Laws are needed in
every society but the great law of the Gospel is the law
of Love.
ARCHBISHOP GUERRY

LET THE GREATER BECOME THE LEAST

Just because we have been raised to the highest level of the hierarchical scale of power which is at work in the Church Militant, we feel that at the same time we have been appointed to the most lowly office of servant of the servants of God. Authority and responsibility, honor and humility, right and duty, power and love, are thereby wonderfully united. We are mindful of the warning of Christ whose vicar we have been appointed, ''He that is greater among you let him become as the younger, as the least, and he that is the leader, as he that serveth'' (Luke 22:26).

FJS

A RELIGION OF WHIMS

We do not want a religion that is right when we are right. What we want is a religion that is right when we are wrong. In these current fashions it is not really a question of the religion allowing us liberty; but (at the best) of the liberty allowing us a religion.... They say they want a religion to be social, when they would be social without any religion. They say they want a religion to be practical, when they would be practical without any religion. They say they want a religion acceptable to science, when they would accept the science even if they did not accept the religion. They say they want a religion like this because they are like this already. They say they want it, when they mean they could do without it.

G. K. CHESTERTON

THE GLORIOUS LIBERTIES

The laws of the Church are not limitations imposed upon us, but rather the gateways to freedom. The Church does not dam up the river of thought; she builds dams to prevent it from overflowing and ruining the countryside of sanity. She does not build great walls around rocky islands in the sea to prevent her children from playing; she builds them to prevent her children from falling into the sea and thus making all play impossible.... We are enslaved if you will, but only at one point. We are slaves to the Kingship of Christ. But that one point is like the fixed point of a pendulum and from it we swing in beautiful rhythm with the freedom of Him Who can do all things. The root of all the liberties of the Church is the most glorious liberty of all—the freedom to become a saint.

FJS

GOODNESS AND MERCY TO ALL

The Catholic Church, lifting high, by means of this Ecumenical Council, the torch of religious truth, intends to show herself as the loving mother of all, benign, patient, full of goodness and mercy, so also to the brothers who are separated from her. To mankind, oppressed by so many difficulties, the Church says as Peter said to the poor who begged him for alms: "I have neither gold nor silver but what I have I give you; in the Name of Christ of Nazareth arise and walk."

POPE JOHN XXIII

101

THE PEOPLE OF CHRIST

It is not a matter for surprise that St. Paul should have
pictured the relations between Christ and His Church
under the image of man and wife. The Church was
the people of Christ, exactly as the Synagogue was the
people of God; and it is a commonplace, when you
are reading the Old Testament prophets, to find Israel
referred to as the Bride of His youth, false to Him now.
"And thou with many lovers hast played the wanton."
So runs the appeal of Jeremiah, "Yet come back to
Me," the Lord says, "and thou shalt find welcome." No
wonder that St. Paul should employ the same kind of
metaphor: "My jealousy on your behalf is the jealousy
of God Himself; I betroth you to Christ, so that no other
but He should claim you, His Bride without spot; and
now I am anxious about you." And so, in writing to the
Ephesians, he represents Our Lord Himself as showing
His love for the Church by giving up His Life for it so
that He might summon it into His Presence, the Church
in all its beauty; it was to be holy, it was to be spotless.
RONALD KNOX

He who has not the Church for a Mother cannot have
God for a Father.
ST. AUGUSTINE

THE
BREAD
FOR
LOVERS
(The Eucharist)

If human love craves oneness, shall not Divine Love? If husband and wife seek to be one in the flesh, shall not the Christian and Christ pray for that oneness with one another? Every heart seeks a happiness outside itself, and since perfect Love is God, then the heart of man and the Heart of Christ must in some way fuse. This aspiration of the soul for its ecstasy is fulfilled in the Eucharist.

FJS

LET CHRIST LIVE IN YOU

What is happening in Holy Communion? What is
happening is that Our Lord is transmitting us into
Himself. In the ordinary way, when we eat something we
are incorporating it into ourselves, making it a part of
ourselves. But in this Heavenly Banquet it is the other
way round. By partaking of the Blessed Sacrament we
do not incorporate It into ourselves; we incorporate
ourselves into It. "I live," St. Paul said long ago, "and
yet it is not exactly I who am living any longer; it would
be more true to say that It is Christ who is living,
continuing the work in me." . . . Are you sure that the
reason why you get so little out of your Communion is
that you put so little into It? You do not receive
because you do not give.

RONALD KNOX

AFTER COMMUNION

Why should I call Thee Lord, Who art my God?
  Why should I call Thee Friend, Who art my Love?
Or King, Who art my very Spouse above?
  Or call Thy Sceptre on my heart Thy rod?
Lo now Thy banner over me is love,
  All heaven flies open to me at Thy nod:
For Thou hast lit Thy flame in me a clod,
  Made me a nest for dwelling of Thy Dove.
  What wilt Thou call me in our home above,
Who now hast called me friend? how will it be
  When Thou for good wine settest forth the best?
Now Thou dost bid me come and sup with Thee,
  Now Thou dost make me lean upon Thy breast:
How will it be with me in time of love?

CHRISTINA GEORGINA ROSSETTI

TO GIVE UP SELF

I wonder, is that why some of us are so frightened of
Holy Communion, because we still cling so to the world
of sense? It is certain that Catholics are most apt to
neglect Communion just when they most need it; in the
springtime of youth, when the blood is hot, and the
passions strong, and ambition dominates us. Why is that,
unless that we are more wedded, when we are young, to
the desires that perish? ... Is it perhaps because, all the
time, we are shrinking from the act of confidence which
would throw the whole burden of our lives on Our Lord;
do not want Holy Communion to have its proper effect
on us, which is to make the joys and distractions of this
world have less meaning and less appeal for us? We must
not expect Him to work the marvels of His grace in us, if
we oppose its actions with the stubbornness of our own
wills, still clinging to self and to sense.

RONALD KNOX

FROM MORTALITY TO IMMORTALITY

As Mary nursed the Child at her breast, maternity was elevated to a kind of natural Eucharist. To every child at her breast, every mother can say : ''Take and eat. This is my body. This is my blood. Unless you eat of my flesh and blood, you shall not have life in you.''

As under the species of Bread day by day Christ nourishes the Christian, so drop by drop the mother nourishes the child. As the Divine Eucharist gives immortality, so this human Eucharist of Motherhood is the guarantee of temporal life. The Angel that once stood at the gates of Paradise to prevent man from eating the Tree of Life now sheathes the sword as life communes both at the altar rail and at a breast. That which in motherhood was first the nourishment of body, with the passage of time becomes the nourishment of mind and soul, as now not drop by drop but word by word, the child is brought closer to the Word, his Savior and his Love.
FJS

COME AND TASTE

There is this difference between spiritual and earthly
pleasures. Before we enjoy them, earthly pleasures are
greatly desired; but when they are partaken to the full,
our liking for them soon begins to pall. Spiritual joys,
on the other hand, are a matter of indifference to us when
we do not possess them, but once we begin to experience
them, we are filled with desire; the more we enjoy them,
the more we desire them. With pleasures of the body, it is
desire that delights us, realization which disappoints;
with pleasures of the soul, desire is weak but spiritual
experience is a source of the greatest joy. . . . When our
souls are full of spiritual joy we long for more, since
by tasting it we learn to desire it more eagerly. We cannot
love what we do not possess, because we do not know its
savour. For who can love what he does not know?
Therefore the Psalmist admonishes us, ''Taste and see
that the Lord is sweet.'' As if he were to say more
explicitly, ''You know not His sweetness if you have
never tasted it; let then your heart but taste the Bread
of Life, that coming to know its sweetness you may be able
to love it.''

ST. GREGORY THE GREAT

THE ECSTASY OF MASS

The Mass is like an engagement, a marriage ceremony and the consummation of the marriage. In the Offertory of the Mass, we become engaged to Christ, inasmuch as we bring gifts of bread and wine as symbols of the offering of ourselves. As the ring is symbol of the lover offering himself to the beloved, so the bread and wine are symbols of the person offering himself to Christ.

After the engagement comes the marriage ceremony in which the lover sacrifices himself for the beloved and the beloved surrenders devotedly to the lover. In the Mass at the moment of Consecration, when the priest says: ''This is My Body and This is My Blood,'' the faithful are now saying: ''This is *my* body; this is *my* blood. Take it. I no longer want it for myself. I am yours.''

In the human order after the engagement and the marriage is the consummation of the marriage. All love craves unity. This is the ecstatic moment in which love becomes too deep for words.

FJS

109

SACRIFICE AND SACRAMENT

The Eucharist is both a Sacrifice and a Sacrament. Does not nature itself have a double aspect: the sacrifice and the sacrament? The vegetables which are served at table, the meat which is presented on the platter, are the natural sacraments of the body of man. By them he lives. If they were endowed with speech, they would say, "Unless you have communion with me, you will not live."

But how do they come to be our sacrament if it was not by sacrifice? Did not the vegetables have to be pulled up by their roots from the earth, submitted to the law of death, then pass through the ordeal of fire, before they could become the sacrament of physical life or have communion with the body?

FJS

BY THE SLAIN CHRIST WE LIVE

A sacrifice must precede a sacrament, as the animal must be sacrificed before it becomes our sacrament. In a certain sense we live by what we slay. Elevating this to the supernatural order, we still live by what we slay. It was our sins that slew Christ on Calvary, and yet it is by Him that we live.

FJS

111

REGAINING LOVE
(Confession)

In psychoanalysis there is the probing by an outside mind; in confession it is the penitent himself who is his own prosecuting attorney and even his own judge. One indispensable condition of receiving pardon is the open avowal of guilt, such as the prodigal son made when he returned again to his father's house.

FJS

PENANCE

Thy hands are washed, but oh the water's spilt,
   That labored to have washed thy guilt;
The flood, if any can, that can suffice,
   Must have its fountains in thine eyes.

RICHARD CRASHAW

CONFESSIONS

In order that there might be a confession, there had to be two miracles: one the creation of a penitent and the other, the creation of a confession. To create a penitent, one had to take man in his pride, enveloped in glacial silence which refuses to unburden his guilt and say to him: ''Thou shalt come to another to confess thy sin.'' The other miracle is to create a confessor. Where find one empowered by God with authority to forgive sins, how train the human heart to heal the wounds of others and then seal his lips forever on what he has learned? Only God could bring these two creations together. There are penitents because there are confessors and there are penitents and confessors because Christ is God.

FJS

"THE DREAM OF GERONTIUS"

When then—if such thy lot—thou seest thy Judge,
The sight of Him will kindle in thy heart
All tender, gracious, reverential thoughts.
Thou wilt be sick with love, and yearn for Him,
And feel as though thou couldst but pity Him,
That one so sweet should e'er have placed Himself
At disadvantage such, as to be used
So vilely by a being so vile as thee.
There is a pleading in His pensive eyes
Will pierce thee to the quick, and trouble thee.
And thou wilt hate and loathe thyself; for, though
Now sinless, thou wilt feel that thou hast sinn'd,
As never thou didst feel; and wilt desire
To slink away, and hide thee from His sight:
And yet wilt have a longing ay to dwell
Within the beauty of His countenance.
And these two pains, so counter and so keen,—
The longing for Him, when thou seest Him not;
The shame of self at thought of seeing him,—
Will be thy veriest, sharpest purgatory.

JOHN HENRY CARDINAL NEWMAN

WHY CONFESSION?

Why did Our Lord demand the telling of sins? Why not bury one's head in one's handkerchief and tell God that one is sorry? Well, if this method of being sorry is not effective when we are caught by a traffic policeman, why should it be effective with God? Shedding tears in one's handkerchief is no test of sorrow, because we are then the judges. Who would ever be sentenced for murder, if everyman was his own judge? How easy it would be for murderers and thieves to escape justice and judgment simply by having a handkerchief ready.

FJS

RECOGNIZING GOOD IN OTHERS

It is a comfortable thought that the smallest and most turbid mud-puddle can contain its own picture of heaven. Let us remember this when we feel inclined to deny all spiritual life to some people, in whom, nevertheless, Our Father may perhaps see the image of His face.

NATHANIEL HAWTHORNE

FREE TO CHOOSE

Now if freedom of choice is, as we believe it to be, an integral part of man's human nature, then it would seem that unless God takes away that freedom, unless, that is to say, man's nature is to be fundamentally changed, such a loss at least seems possible. So long, therefore, as man is a free agent he must be free to reject the sovereignty of God; and God will not *compel* him to accept it. Man can fight his own perfection. He can deliberately choose to remain outside the love of God. . . . That this power of choice may be lost, and lost forever, is, in part at least, that which underlies the doctrine of Hell. The will can be fixed in antagonism to God.

FRANK BIGEART

HEAVEN OR HELL

Alone, O Love ineffable!
   Thy saving name is given;
To turn aside from Thee is hell
   To walk with Thee is heaven!

JOHN GREENLEAF WHITTIER

"GODDESS OF MERCY"

There is a beautiful legend of Kwan-yin, the Chinese goddess of mercy, to whom so many pleadings have gone forth from Chinese lips. According to the legend, this princess lived in China hundreds of years before Christ was born. Her father, the king, wished her to marry, but, resolving upon a life of virginity, she took refuge in the convent. Her angry father burned the convent and forced her to return to his palace. Given the alternative of death or marriage, she insisted on her vow of virginity, and so her father strangled her. Her body was brought to hell by a tiger. It was there she won the title "goddess of mercy." Her intercession for mercy was so great, and she so softened the hard hearts of hell, that the very devils ordered her to leave. They were afraid she would empty hell. She then returned to an island off the coast of Cheking where, even to this day, pilgrims travel to her shrine. The Chinese at times pictured her as wearing on her head the image of God, to whose heaven she brings the faithful, although she herself refuses to enter heaven, so long as there is a single soul excluded.

FJS

THE PRICE OF LOVE REJECTED

What is hell? It is the suffering that comes from being
unable to love. Once in an infinite existence that cannot
be measured in time or space, a spiritual creature,
appearing on earth, was given the ability to say, "I am,
and I love." Once, and only once, he was given a moment
of active, living love, and it was for that that he received
earthly life with its temporal limitations. But that happy
being did not appreciate and welcome the priceless gift;
he rejected it, looking at it perversely and unmoved. He
goes loveless before God to draw near to those who have
loved when he has despised their love. . . . They cursed
God in life and now they are themselves accursed. They
feed on their malignant pride like a man starving in the
desert who sucks blood from his own veins. But they can
never have enough, never and they spurn forgiveness,
cursing the God Who called them. They cannot look upon
the Living God without hating Him and they wish that
the God of Life could be no more, that He would destroy
Himself and all His Creation. They will burn eternally in
the flames of their own rage, longing for death and
nothingness. But there will be no death for them.
DOSTOEVSKI

AVOWAL OF GUILT

In Confession and in psychoanalysis the disturbed mind seeks to throw off its burden. As Shakespeare put it: "My tongue will tell the anger of my heart, or else my heart concealing it, will break." But there is a difference between the two. Psychoanalysis is the avowal of an attitude of mind; confession is an avowal of guilt. A person can be proud of the state of mind, boasting that he is an atheist or immoral. But no one can be proud of his guilt, when he says, "I am responsible for this evil."

FJS

Hell is the final barring of the last rampart against the love of God.

FJS

WHERE LOVE IS NOT

Why this is Hell, nor am I out of it
Thinkest thou that I, who saw the Face of God,
And tasted the eternal joys of heaven,
Am not tormented with ten thousand hells
In being deprived of everlasting bliss? ...

When all the world dissolves,
And every creature shall be purified,
All places shall be Hell that are not Heaven.

MEPHISTOPHELES IN MARLOWE'S FAUST

MARRIED LOVE

Marriages do not endure because people fall in love with an ecstasy or a thrill, loving the cake only as long as it has frosting on it.
FJS

HUMAN LOVE

The human love of married persons is powerless to
engender other than the children of the old Adam. The
increase of their offspring, more and more divided from
one another with the succeeding generations, serves but
to extend the sphere of death. Mary, renouncing human
love, gave birth to the new Adam, and, in Him, all the
children of the old Adam are enabled to attain eternal
life, the very life of God. So it is that God will finally
consummate His union with mankind of which the union
of man and woman was simply the image.

LOUIS BOUYER

MARRIAGE

That there should exist one other person in the world
towards whom all openness of exchange should establish
itself, from whom there should be no concealment; whose
body should be as dear to one, in every part, as one's
own; with whom there should be no sense of mine or
thine, in property or possession; into whose mind one's
thoughts should naturally flow, as it were to know
themselves and receive a new illumination; and between
whom and oneself there should be a spontaneous rebound
of sympathy in all the joys and sorrows and experiences of
life; such is perhaps one of the dearest wishes of the soul.

EDWARD CARPENTER

LOVE IS ETERNAL

To those who are conscious of spiritual realities it seems
more consonant with truth to think of love, not as
derived from sex, but as an ultimate value revealed
through the workings of sex. Sex is a human happening
in time and space. Love is eternal in the heavens : but
sex provides the medium through which love's earthly
work can be accomplished and such work is creative on all
its planes.

E. D. HUTCHINSON

RENOUNCEMENT

Married love has its moments of renouncement, whether
they be dictated by nature or by the absence of the
beloved. If nature impose a sacrifice and asceticism on
married love by force, why should not grace freely
suggest a virgin love ? What one does out of the exigencies
of time, the other does out of the exigencies of eternity.
Every act of love is an engagement for the future, but the
virgin's vow centers more on eternity than on time.

FJS

HONORABLE WEDDED LIVES

And wedded lives, which not belie
The honorable heart of love,
Are fountains of virginity.

COVENTRY PATMORE

125

PROPOSAL

My darling Jeanne, my sweet betrothed, you are my consolation, my sole hope after God, who threw you into my arms. Here are true words come from the bottom of the heart of that proud fellow : I am a man who is very poor, very unhappy, very weak, very ill, very forsaken. I am the least among the destitute, a being who is trampled, a man dying of thirst for love. If you should happen to fail me, everything at once would fail me. I love your soul, your mind, your body, and I hope that all this will be given to me, because we shall marry, because I have an infinite need for you, because you have been offered to me and—I have not sought you. Your protection is necessary to me, and that protection, my God ! must not hold off too long, for I feel as though I were dying.

LÉON BLOY

LOVE LETTER TO A FUTURE WIFE

Your letter arrived this afternoon : I got it at five o'clock, and put it unopened in my pocket, got on my bicycle and rode out into the country. I felt I must read it alone and with God. I will show you the place one day. Then I raised my heart in prayer to God, as I have been doing many times each day since the day at Brindisi. I had utterly committed the whole matter to Him. In the quiet light of the setting sun, I broke the seal and saw the ''Yes.'' I bowed my head and took you from the Hands of God : then gave yourself and myself back to Him to fulfill His utter will. Please God these things will make something heavenly, something spiritual and ethereal in our relations one to another. Something that God may have pleasure in and use to His own glory.

TEMPLE GAIRDNER

THE BEAUTY OF COMMUNICATING

... Even in human relationships speech is simply a
necessary part of fellowship. We all know, for example,
marriages in which the couples no longer speak to each
other. Such marriages are dead relationships, bleak ruins
of a love long since lost, even though they have not been
divorced. A living relationship requires speech, the *word,*
interchange. . . . The depth of friendship proves itself by
the length of time one can be silent with each other
without feeling that the silence is painful,— this is
eloquent silence. This eloquent silence indicates the
degree of fellowship in which there is a continuing
interchange and intercommunication, which no longer
needs to be expressed in spoken words because the waves
of an inner, inaudible conversation are constantly playing
back and forth.

HELMUT THIELICKE

LOOK TO YOURSELF

To give advice is to place oneself above one's fellow,
thereby obstructing the spiritual fellowship in which
alone he can be helped. The best way to help one's wife
or husband to make headway in life is to go ahead oneself.
When the children become particularly difficult, the
parents have only to ask themselves what is wrong
within, and to correct that. I see many people who would
like to solve a marital problem before having solved their
most elementary personal problem. . . . Real problems are
not between them but in each of the partners themselves.
PAUL TOURNIER

129

FAITH

*Homer, a thousand years before Christ, threw
into the stream of history the mystery of a
woman faithful in sorrow and loneliness. While
her husband, Ulysses, was away on his travels,
Penelope was courted by many suitors. She told
them she would marry one of them when she
finished weaving a garment. But each night she
undid the stitches she had put in during the day,
and thus she remained faithful until her husband
returned. No one who sang the song of Homer
could understand why he glorified the sorrowful
mother, as they could not understand why, in
another poem, he glorified the defeated hero. It
was not for a thousand years, until the day of
a defeated Hero on a Cross, and a Sorrowful
Mother beneath it, that the world understood
the mysteries of Homer.*
FJS

FAITH'S EVENTUAL VICTORY

During the war, there was a countrywoman in France
who hid a Chinese Communist. He tried to undermine her
faith, she answered him, "You are a learned man, you
have studied a lot; all I know is that Jesus told us to love
others as He loved them." One day a number of fugitives,
Communists too, fleeing from the German advance,
asked this woman for shelter. She gave them her room,
and went to sleep in the passage, after giving them all the
bed clothes she had. Very early the next day they stole
away, taking everything with them. The Chinaman
was furious, and watched the woman carefully, but saw
not the slightest sign of anger. He then and there decided
to become a Catholic and is now a priest all through the
acts of one poor woman.

CHARLES JOURNET

FAITH STRENGTHENS TRUST

Put thy trust in God,
Let Him be thy fear and thy love.
He shall answer for thee
And will do in all things what is best for thee.

THOMAS A KEMPIS

132

FAITH AND KNOWLEDGE

The knowledge of faith, if the heart carries through and
follows the movement of the eyes, is not only the evoking
of the object but an intimate conversation with Someone,
a converse with a welcome Guest, a dialog with the
Beloved. In faith, there is embryonically centered the
whole contemplative and mystic life—in fact a man's
entire life of blessed happiness.

FATHER DE LA MOTTE

FAITH, NATURE AND GOD

There is no unbelief;
Whoever plants a seed beneath the sod
And waits to see it push away the clod,
He trusts in God.

Whoever says when clouds are in the sky,
Be patient, heart, light breaketh by and by,
Trusts the Most High.

Whoever sees neath the field of winter snow,
The silent harvest of the future grow
God's power must know.

EDWARD BULWER-LYTTON

FAITH AS A RESTORER

Among all my patients in the second half of life—that is
to say, over thirty-five—there has not been one whose
problem in the last resort was not that of finding a
religious outlook on life. It is safe to say that every one
of them fell ill because he had lost that which the living
religions of every age have given to their followers and
none of them has been really healed who did not regain
his religious outlook.

C. G. JUNG

FAITH AND TRUTHS

Everyone who believes assents to someone's words; and
thus, in any form of belief, it seems that it is *the person
to whose words the assent is given* who is of principal
importance, and, as it were, the end; while the individual
truths through which one assents to that person are
secondary.

THOMAS AQUINAS

WHAT IS FAITH?

Faith is the response of the human person to the Personal
God, and thus it is the *meeting of two persons.* In the
act of faith the *whole* man is involved.

JEAN MOUROUX

TO GOD THE FATHER

It is centuries since I believed in you,
  But today my need of You has come back.
I want no rose-coloured future,
  No books of learning, no protestations and denials—
I am sick of this ugly scramble,
  I am tired of being pulled about—
O God, I want to sit on Your knees
  On the all-too-big throne of Heaven,
And fall asleep with my hands tangled in your gray beard.

KATHERINE MANSFIELD

FAITH AND REGENERATION

The creative action of the Holy Spirit in applying the
Gospel Message is seen in the fact that the sinner enters
into a new moral universe with new moral powers, as he
passes from the stage of conviction to that of
regeneration.

E. Y. MULLINS

LOST FAITH

Jung's approach is closely in line with what I have been
saying. He claims that side by side with the decline of the
religious life comes the increase in neurosis.

GORDON ALLPORT

FAITH, THE CONVERTER

Asia and the ancient world had an air of being too old to die. Christendom has had the very opposite fate. Christendom has had a series of revolutions and in each one of them Christianity has died. Christianity has died many times and risen again; for it had a God Who knew the way out of the grave. But the first extraordinary fact which marks this history is this. That Europe has been turned upside down over and over again; and that at the end of each of these revolutions the same religion has again been found on top. The Faith is always converting the age, not as an old religion but as a new religion. . . . Christianity is not going to remain as a ghost. What follows this process of apparent death is not the lingering of a shade; it is the resurrection of the body. These people are quite prepared to shed pious reverential tears over the sepulchre of the Son of Man; what they are not prepared for is the Son of Man walking once more upon the hills of the morning.

G. K. CHESTERTON

Saints never deny Hell; they fear it. Unrepentant sinners never fear it; they deny it.

FJS

FAITH'S FOUNDATION

In the history of the world, only one tomb has ever had a
rock rolled before it, and a soldier guard set to watch it
to prevent the dead Man within from rising; that was
the tomb of Christ on the evening of the Friday called
Good. What spectacle could be more ridiculous than
armed soldiers keeping their eyes on a Corpse? But
sentinels were set, lest the dead walk, the silent speak,
and the pierced Heart quicken to the throb of life. They
said He was dead; they knew He was dead; they said He
would never rise again, and yet they watched! In His
Resurrection He has given the earth its most serious
wound—the empty tomb. And to us our greatest hope.

FJS

STEADFAST FAITH

It seems to me that there is a great change come over the
world since people like US believed in God, God is now
gone for all of us. Yet we must believe. And not only that,
we must carry our weakness and our sin and our
devilishness to Somebody. I don't mean in a bad, abasing
way. But we must feel that we are *known,* that our hearts
are known as God knew us.

KATHERINE MANSFIELD

GROWTH OF FAITH

There are three stages of faith : (1) When we simply
accept the teaching of the Church without reflecting
upon it, or understanding why it is worthy of belief; (2)
When our reason approves our faith; (3) When we
experience inwardly what we have believed . . . in this
mystic experience the Christian comes into perfect union
with God, a union mediated by both love and knowledge.
HUGO OF ST. VICTOR

One of the first activities of the believing person is to
distinguish between the purely intellectual assent and
the subjective appropriation of truth.
ROBERT O. FERM

INDEX
OF
AUTHORS